P9-BZQ-603

21 Strategies for Improving Employee Communication

for Communicators

By the staff of **Davis & Company**
Edited by **Alison Davis**

Davis & Company, Inc.
11 Harristown Road
Glen Rock, NJ 07452
Phone: (201) 445-5100
www.davisandco.com

Davis & Company is the leader in employee communication consulting and implementation. With more than 20 years of experience helping companies reach, engage and motivate employees, Davis & Company creates innovative processes, programs and vehicles that dramatically improve the success of employee communication.

Book design by Davis & Company
Graphic design by Janice Comes
1st edition
Printed in the United States of America

© 2005 by Davis & Company

All rights reserved. No part of this book may be reproduced in any form or by any means without written permission from Davis & Company, except for the inclusion of brief quotations in a review.

ISBN 0-9713061-8-4

Contents

Introduction

If your responsibilities include employee communication, this book is for you.

21 Strategies for Improving Employee Communication is designed to provide practical advice on seven aspects of employee communication: Planning, Measurement, Communicating Change, Leaders' and Managers' Communication, Print and Electronic Communication Channels, Visual Communication and the Communication Function.

Each strategy has been adapted from the archives of our acclaimed electronic newsletter, *Smart Tips*. Since 2002, *Smart Tips* has provided more than 3,000 subscribers with 26 issues a year of hands-on tips they can put to work immediately. Each *Smart Tips* issue takes just minutes to read, yet subscribers tell us that the information is valuable and useful.

If your mission is to communicate effectively with employees, you know that you can't accept the status quo: you must constantly re-examine your strategies, and continually make improvements in your approaches. This book, which is built on Davis & Company's extensive employee communication experience, is designed to help.

Subscribe to *Smart Tips*

If you're interested in subscribing to our award-winning electronic newsletter, visit our website at **www.davisandco.com**

Communicators like you have told us that these are some of the issues that keep them up at night:

"**No one is reading what we send.** They're deleting e-mails without opening them. They don't remember important communication. How can we break through the clutter and **get through to people?**"

"How can we reach a **global, diverse workforce?**"

"For our organization to be successful, **we need employees to understand the strategy/brand** and know how to do their jobs to support it."

The challenge of communicating effectively

We provide advice for communicators because we know how challenging employee communication has become—we've been doing it for more than two decades. Twenty years ago, it was relatively easy to reach employees. Companies and their workers had long-term relationships that served as an "employment contract": Organizations offered job security, and employees, in turn, gave their loyalty and attention. But workplace changes—mergers, downsizing, outsourcing, etc. have broken the bond between company and worker. Today, employees are skeptical; they question what companies have to communicate.

A new approach to communication

To get through to today's employees, you need to compete with all the other demands on their time and attention. Employees need to be convinced that internal communication is just as compelling, interesting, credible and useful as what they can find on the Internet, on CNN or in the newspaper.

In fact, employee communication has to be better than external media—employees need to believe they can get more relevant information and deeper meaning through internal channels than they can get anywhere else.

The old way of communicating—top-down, "journalistic," corporate, static, staid—doesn't work. Unless you take a radically different approach, you will not succeed at engaging employees.

"**How do we know that our communication is working?** How do we measure/demonstrate its effectiveness?"

"We communicate so much that the information people receive is sometimes **redundant, confusing and even contradictory** (for example, corporate vs. divisional messages). How do we create alignment? **What can we do to develop a sense of priorities?**"

We give you lots of advice in the pages ahead, but here are four strategies to get started:

1. **Don't underestimate the media's influence.** Communicators can't assume that they are an employee's sole source for company information. The increase in access to various forms of media (Internet, AP releases, 24-hour news coverage) has given employees the ability to search for information, get multiple viewpoints about a subject, or even join a chat group about their company. But as a communicator, you can share perspectives that will help employees understand what all the data really means. And you can provide context in a way the media simply can't match.

2. **Treat employees as consumers.** Employees used to wait eagerly for the next memo or issue of the newsletter. But as a result of proliferation of media (see #1 above), employees are no longer a captive audience. To respond, you need to think about what will appeal to employees. How can you hold their interest? How do you answer the eternal questions: "What does this mean to me?" and "What do I do about this?"

3. **Communicate with candor**. Your employees don't want information that's sugarcoated. In fact, they can detect "spin" from a mile away. As one employee in a recent focus group told us, "It feels like all the communication is marketing. It doesn't give us the straight story." Be sure communication is as candid as possible (given the constraints of legal and regulatory issues).

4 **Make it easy for employees to feel proud of the company.** The bottom line is that there will always be a relationship between employers and employees. And while that relationship may be changing, communication can support and, perhaps, strengthen that bond. Leverage the fact that employees want to feel proud of working at your company, and feel that their work is contributing to the company's success. Build pride through your communication: share good news, highlight success stories and talk about the positive aspects of the company.

Your employees today:

Your employee population is not a captive audience. In fact, it's likely that employees in your organization:

- **Are not waiting expectantly for the next message from senior management**
- **Don't believe everything the company tells them—in some cases, they don't believe anything they hear**
- **Are too busy to browse the intranet just to learn about the company or an important issue**
- **Expect to learn immediately what the message means to them and what they should do about it**
- **Feel free to tune out by hitting the e-mail delete button, throwing the newsletter unread into the recycling bin, skipping quickly over the home page, or multi-tasking while listening to the CEO's webcast**

In short, they are savvy media consumers who want to control their communication experience.

Get started today

If you're like most communicators we meet,
the good news is you're smart, creative and experienced. The bad news is you're very, very busy, to the point of overload.

Don't forget to eat right and get a good night's sleep. And then steal a few minutes out of your day to read some of the tips in this book—we're sure they'll inspire you, stimulate your thinking and give you advice you can use to improve your program today.

The result? Employees will be informed and involved. The organization will be energized. Senior management will be satisfied. And your success will be assured.

Communication Planning

What did George Patton say about planning?

A | "A goal without a plan is just a wish."

B | "It is bad planning that admits of no modification."

C | "A man, a plan, a canal, Panama."

D | "A good plan, violently executed now, is better than a perfect plan next week."

E | None of the above

For answer, see page 16

Give Your Plan a Consistent Framework

Tired of reinventing the wheel every time you develop a communication plan? By creating a consistent approach to planning, the process will be easier and more productive. All it takes is a simple planning framework.

Why a planning framework is important

The purpose of a planning framework isn't to impose rigid guidelines, but to identify key components to include in all of your company's communication plans, and guide you through each step of the planning process. In addition to simplifying your approach, a planning framework:

- **Aligns communication efforts.** You and your colleagues can leverage the same planning framework to coordinate communication activities throughout local business units and the company as a whole.
- **Sets clear expectations.** All communicators in your company, regardless of job level or location, will understand what the key components of a plan are and how to deliver on them.

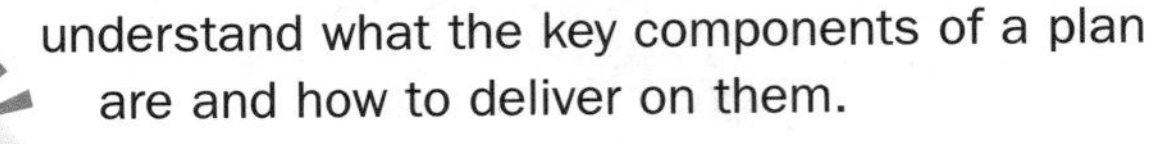

How you can build a planning framework

1. **Establish key components.** While there isn't a magic number of components to include in your framework, here are some you should consider:

   Objectives. Specific outcomes you hope to achieve

   Strategies. Methods or approaches for achieving your objectives

   Tactics. Tools you'll use or actions you'll take

   Audience/Stakeholders. Individuals or groups to reach

   Roles. Communication responsibilities of key players including leaders, managers, peers, etc.

   Timing. Specific times/dates for completing tasks

2. **Articulate these components in a written template.** Your template doesn't need to be elaborate or fancy. A simple Microsoft® Office Word document will do the trick. You and your colleagues could leverage the template to develop the annual communication plan, as well as refer to it when developing individual project plans throughout the year.

Keep your plans simple

Make it brief. Most communication plans are too long and, therefore, too overwhelming for people to read. (No one has time to plow through a 50-page document.) Instead, write more simply and succinctly. Focus on the key points in each section and use bullets and subheads to break up chunks of text.

Write in a conversational tone. As with all your writing, avoid jargon and "corporate speak" that weigh documents down. Stick to conversational language to which people can relate.

Consider "quick read" formats. Instead of formatting your plan in a bound, narrative document, create a brief "landscape" Microsoft® Office Word document or in Microsoft® Office PowerPoint®, using few words and many graphics. These formats encourage you to be brief and they also display horizontal images, such as timelines, more easily.

2

Use Situation Analysis and Principles

Create a strong foundation for your communication plan by considering situational analysis and communication principles. A focused situational analysis not only builds a strong foundation for your plan, it also helps you make a case for your objectives, strategies and tactics. And communication principles will give your messages, activities and plans context and consistency.

What is it?

It may seem obvious, but a situation analysis is just what it seems: it's a summary of a situation—a snapshot that conveys what's going on at that moment in time.

Creating a situation analysis

Bring together your team, or the people you're working with on the communication plan, to think collaboratively about the current climate in your organization. Through this dialogue, consider the following questions:

- Why is this plan being developed?
- What is the current state of communication within the organization?
- What is the current state of the organization (reorganization, merger, etc.)?
- What are the organization's goals or strategies?
- What must employees understand to achieve those goals?

What's included

A situation analysis typically addresses the contributing factors for creating a communication plan, including:

- **Recent organizational changes** (structural or staffing)
- **Rollout of new corporate goals/objectives**
- **Changing market** or industry dynamics
- **New expectations** for employees to work differently

Communication principles enhance your plan

The next time you create a communication plan, think about articulating your communication principles as part of the process. These are your beliefs about how communication should happen within your organization and they set the stage for the rest of the planning process.

Communication principles are an important part of the planning process. They:

- Shape your strategies
- Demonstrate your rationale for proposing certain tactics

Your communication principles should be unique to your organization's culture and values. There are no rules about how many you create: some companies articulate two or three general principles that guide all employee communication, while others develop 10 or more and tailor them each time they create a plan for a big initiative/event.

Sample principles

"We tell the truth."

"We communicate first to employees who are significantly affected by an event/change."

"If we don't know the whole story or can't share it, we tell people what we can and let them know when they'll hear more."

"Dialogue is our first choice for communication."

Gain Buy-in Faster

Once you've finalized your annual communication plan, your next likely step is to share it with others. But due to the minute detail involved in most plans, sharing it can be overwhelming both for you and the recipients. Even in a boiled-down slide presentation, you may notice people's eyes glazing over after the fifth or sixth strategy. What can you do?

The solution is to create a one-page visual "map" or "graph" of your plan. The best approach for this is an 11"x17", full color, nicely designed sheet that depicts major components of your plan. The main benefit of making your plan visual is that it allows you to take it on the road, talk through it quickly and, since most adults are visual learners, gain buy-in more readily. The visual is also easily posted on a wall to keep you and your team focused on your stated mission, objectives and tactics.

INTERNAL COMMUNICATIONS PLAN AT A GLANCE

INTERNAL COMMUNICATIONS MISSION

The mission of Internal Communications is to create and facilitate clear and engaging communication that contributes to the Company's success and is useful and meaningful to associates.

COMMUNICATION PRINCIPLES

Communication at the Company supports our values and follows these principles:

Integrity
- Tell the truth

Excellence
- Use the right communication tool for the right job
- Make communication interesting
- Create clear, concise, consistent and contextual messages

Accountability
- Make communication the responsibility of every associate
- Help people understand what to do
- Respect people's time

Diversity
- Communicate consistently globally
- Adapt communication for local needs
- Communicate so associates understand, "what this means to me"

Teamwork
- Create dialogue
- Encourage feedback and questions
- Facilitate communication between groups and individuals

OBJECTIVES By the end of the year

Associates will be introduced to and understand:
- The current business environment and why the Company must change to compete
- The Company's ambitions and objectives
- The Company's strategic direction
- The Company's performance and progress

Associates will understand what is expected of them at work.

Senior leaders, key leaders and managers will understand their communication role and be supported to fulfill that role.

Associates will be satisfied with internal communication vehicles and channels.

Associates will be actively involved in the communication process.

STRATEGIES

1. Support senior leaders, key leaders and managers to help them understand and fulfill their communication roles.
2. Create a message platform that sets priorities and puts information into context.
3. Leverage and enhance current communication vehicles.
4. Honor heritage and celebrate accomplishments.
5. Make communication participative through dialogue and feedback.
6. Assess communication needs and effectiveness.

COMMUNICATION ROLES

INTERNAL COMMUNICATIONS
- Engage associates in communication through dialogue
- Establish communication protocols and guidelines
- Raise the standard of communication within the organization

THE ORGANIZATION

SENIOR LEADERS
- Communicate a consistent and compelling Company story:
  - Goals/aspirations
  - Strategies
  - Performance
- Explain how the big picture connects to his/her area or function
- Celebrate success

KEY LEADERS
- Understand and share the Company story as it relates to his/her function/area
- Communicate how the Company's direction affects:
  - Group goals/aspirations
  - Group strategies
  - Group performance

MANAGERS
- Understand and share how changes in the group and function/area impact the work team and individual associates
- Communicate how the Company's direction affects:
  - Team and individual goals/aspirations
  - Team and individual strategies
  - Team and individual performance

ASSOCIATES
- Understand how his/her performance connects to the team and group
- Provide ongoing feedback to managers and leaders

KEY MESSAGES

Key messages are the main themes that Internal Communications will focus on in the coming year. These messages will provide context and clarity to help manage the changes affecting the Company.

Our key messages are:

To achieve success in the constantly evolving environment, the Company is:
- Following a new Strategic Direction—why and how the company is changing
- Improving its systems and processes
- Building a strong culture
- Developing and nurturing its people
- Celebrating its accomplishments

SUPPORTING ROLE OF EACH VEHICLE

Leader Meeting:

Intranet

All Company Briefing:

Newsletter:

Manager Website:

Executive Tour:

Manager Briefing

Here are some tips for creating a great visual of your plan:

- **Think about your audience.** Will they be most concerned with your objectives and strategies, or roles and tactics? Create your visual map accordingly and keep in mind, you may need to do different visual depictions for different audiences.
- **Design matters.** This is one case where it pays to bring in a professional designer who can help you lay out your one-pager in the most appealing way. Sketch it out for the designer so he/she clearly understands the goal of the visual and how it will be used.
- **Keep it simple.** Stick to the top-line details of your plan. You can always pull out the big, bound document if someone wants more information.

Case studies

How two leading companies have used one-page visual depictions of their plans:

- **A pharmaceutical company** needed to share the main components of its annual plan with a global team, so its visual included the communication mission and principles, the plan's objectives, communication roles for leaders and managers, and key strategies all on one page.
- **A research consulting company** needed to outline its planned tactics, so it developed a calendar where each month outlined key tactics and an icon system linking tactics to key strategies.

3 things to remember about communication planning:

1. **Establish a consistent framework** for communication plans to make them easier to create and more uniform.
2. **Develop a situation analysis** to build a foundation and rationale for your objectives, strategies and tactics.
3. **Make your plan visual** to sell it to key stakeholders.

Answer to question on page 9

D | "A good plan, violently executed now, is better than a perfect plan next week."

amazon.com

Returns Are Easy!

Visit http://www.amazon.com/returns to return any item - including gifts - in unopened or original condition within 30 days for a full refund (other restrictions apply). Please have your order ID ready.

Your order of March 8, 2011 (Order ID 104-2862078-3869828)

Qty.	Item	Item Price	Tota
1	**21 Strategies for Improving Employee Communication** Staff of Davis & Company --- Paperback **(** P-1-C19D204 **) 0971306184**	$19.95	$19.9

This shipment completes your order.

Have feedback on how we packaged your order? Tell us at www.amazon.com/packaging.

Subtotal	$19.9
Shipping & Handling	$3.9
Order Total	$23.94
Paid via Amex	$23.94
Balance due	$0.0

13/Dgws4wJqR/-1 of 1-//1SS/std-n-us/7235640/0310-12:30/0309-15:23

B2A

Measuring Communication

What's the first rule of communication measurement?

A | Measure twice, cut once

B | What gets measured gets done

C | A stitch in time saves nine

D | Marry in haste, repent in leisure

E | All of the above

For answer, see page 24

Make Questions Your Foundation

Twenty years ago, most communicators did not measure the effectiveness of their efforts; today, "metrics" have become a must, as senior leaders demand accountability and communicators seek to explore the impact on employees. Luckily, as the importance of measurement has increased, so have methodology choices—from simple print questionnaires to interactive online surveys that "respond" to participants' answers and ask relevant follow-up questions. Despite these advancements, the foundation of successful measurement remains effective questions.

Writing effective survey questions has always been both a science—market researchers extensively study how people respond to the wording of questions—and an art. Here's how to create survey questions that are direct, simple and specific:

- **Create clear objectives.** Objectives are the platform upon which every research study is based. Before you can begin writing questions, you need to articulate what you are trying to learn as a result of your research. Define three to five outcomes—what you will learn—as a result of your measurement effort. Use these objectives as a framework for the questions you create.

- **Decide on the type of information you are seeking.**
  Most survey questions ask about one of four attributes:

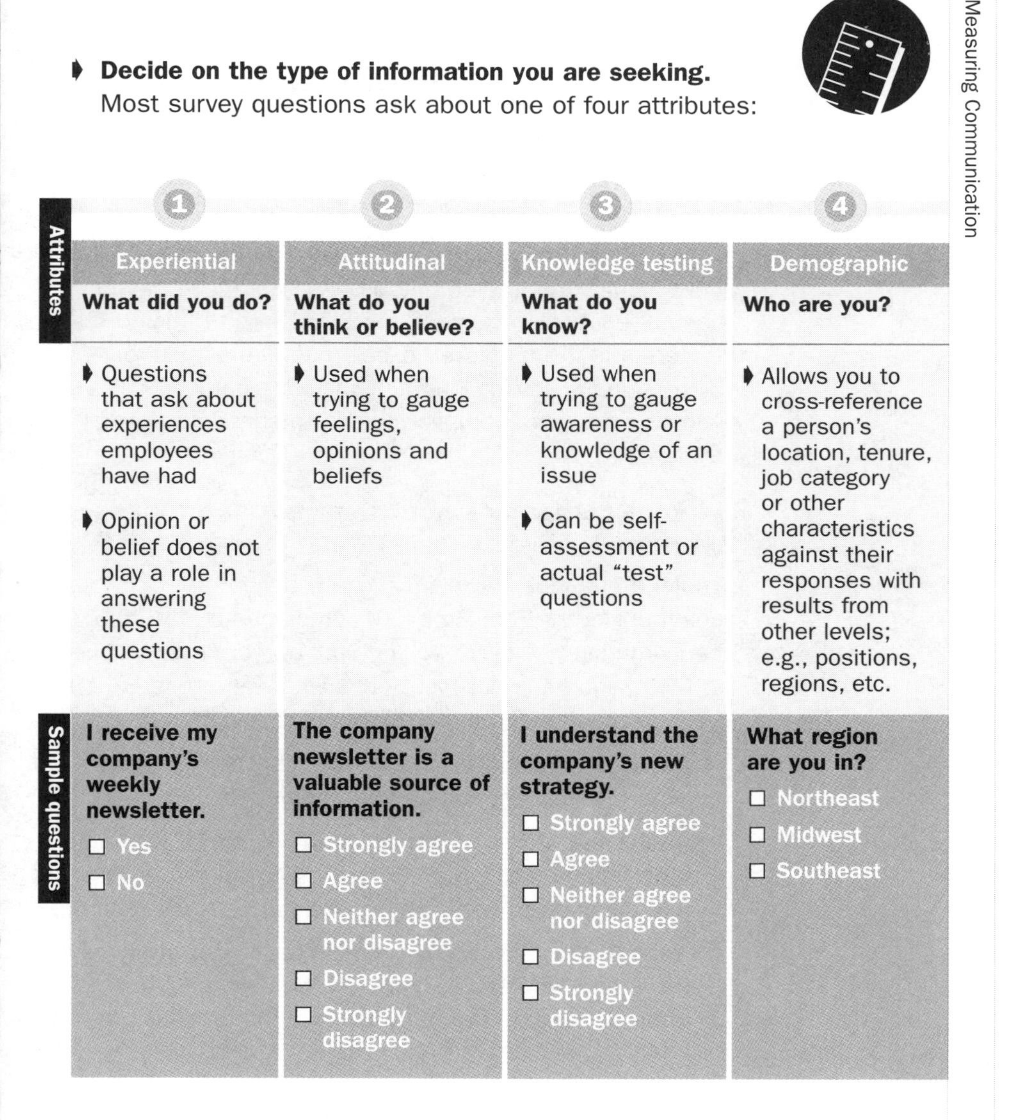

	1 Experiential	2 Attitudinal	3 Knowledge testing	4 Demographic
Attributes	**What did you do?**	**What do you think or believe?**	**What do you know?**	**Who are you?**
	• Questions that ask about experiences employees have had • Opinion or belief does not play a role in answering these questions	• Used when trying to gauge feelings, opinions and beliefs	• Used when trying to gauge awareness or knowledge of an issue • Can be self-assessment or actual "test" questions	• Allows you to cross-reference a person's location, tenure, job category or other characteristics against their responses with results from other levels; e.g., positions, regions, etc.
Sample questions	**I receive my company's weekly newsletter.** ☐ Yes ☐ No	**The company newsletter is a valuable source of information.** ☐ Strongly agree ☐ Agree ☐ Neither agree nor disagree ☐ Disagree ☐ Strongly disagree	**I understand the company's new strategy.** ☐ Strongly agree ☐ Agree ☐ Neither agree nor disagree ☐ Disagree ☐ Strongly disagree	**What region are you in?** ☐ Northeast ☐ Midwest ☐ Southeast

5

Evaluate Effectiveness of Print Distribution

It's dangerous to assume you know how effectively your print publication is distributed based on anecdotes or casual feedback. You need hard evidence to fully understand the employee experience and adjust your distribution approach to reach changing demographics. The only way to accomplish this is to conduct a formal evaluation.

Is your company's print distribution process working?

That's a question Davis & Company asked communicators from 25 major companies in our 2005 benchmarking study, *Reaching Employees: Best Practices in Distribution and Access*. Here's what we learned about how companies distribute their print publications:

Most communicators can verify that their company-wide print publication has been shipped.

About half of the communicators we spoke with said they include a question or two in an annual survey related to employees' perceptions of print distribution.

None of the companies represented in our study have a systematic metrics approach for evaluating the effectiveness of their print distribution process.

Why you need to evaluate print distribution

Are you overlooking the importance of evaluating how effectively your print publication is distributed? While you can create a compelling, award-winning publication, it's meaningless if no one picks it up and reads it. Without evaluating print distribution, you:

- Don't know if your work is meeting the needs of employees
- Can't develop meaningful plans
- Are unable to demonstrate the impact of your work to senior management

How to evaluate your print distribution process

There are various methods for evaluating print distribution. As with all forms of research, the deeper you dig, the richer your findings will be. Here are a couple of techniques to consider:

1 | **Conduct a survey.** At the very least, you should conduct an annual survey to measure vehicle effectiveness. Part of your survey should include questions about employees' perceptions of print distribution. Sample questions include:

- **Do you have access to the company-wide print publication?**
- **How do you receive it?**
- **How effective is the distribution process?**

2 | **Observe how print distribution is working.** One observation method that market researchers commonly use to examine consumer behavior is called "The Mystery Shopper." The way it works is an individual enters a store disguised as an ordinary shopper to observe the customer experience.

You can replicate this method in your own organization by observing what happens when a new edition of the print publication arrives at your facility. Does every employee receive a copy? How long does the distribution process take? Do employees generally read the publication right away or file it away for a later time? Do employees bring the publication home with them or recycle it at the facility?

Go Beyond Hits When Measuring Intranet Usage

Do you really know how employees are using your company's intranet? If your only measurement tool is a hit report, you're not getting the full story. To truly understand intranet usage, go beyond hits and dig deeper, with advanced usage reports and employee research.

The problem with hits

Hit reports have some value tracking activity around intranet usage. However, they don't go far enough to provide a detailed analysis of how visitors are really using your site. Take a look at the following hit report from a company with 25,000 employees with online access:

Hits per month: 50,000

Could mean...	Or...
All 25,000 employees with online access visited two pages each	250 employees with online access visited an average of 200 pages each

Advanced tracking systems

Fortunately, there are a variety of advanced systems that offer a wider range of tracking options. For the most part, these systems are fairly easy and cost-effective to set up. Talk with your IT group about the different options available to you.

Dive deeper to know your audiences

As with all forms of research, the deeper you dive, the richer your findings will be. Here are additional strategies to help you fully understand if you're meeting employees' needs:

1. **Conduct a survey.** If you conduct an annual survey to measure vehicle effectiveness, you should include questions on intranet usage. Make sure your survey questions reflect the functions your intranet was designed to fulfill. Here are some sample questions:

Sample survey questions

I am able to navigate through the intranet with ease.
☐Strongly agree ☐Agree ☐Neutral ☐Disagree ☐Strongly disagree

The intranet contains the information I need to do my job.
☐Strongly agree ☐Agree ☐Neutral ☐Disagree ☐Strongly disagree

I use the intranet to learn more about the markets in which we operate.
☐Strongly agree ☐Agree ☐Neutral ☐Disagree ☐Strongly disagree

2. **Hold user tests.** User testing is one of the most reliable ways to measure intranet usage because the results are based on actual experience vs. perceptions. A typical user test consists of a select group of employees who perform tasks on the intranet while others observe their behavior. Some of the information gathered through user tests include:

   How fast do users complete a given task?

   What paths do they take in trying?

   Where do they stumble? What problems do they have?

   Do users typically click through pages or do they use the search function?

   How do they react to the download time for specific pages?

3 things to remember about measuring communication:

1. **Set clear objectives** for your research study, then create questions that will meet those objectives.

2. **Include questions** about distribution in your annual communication survey.

3. **Don't rely solely on hits** to measure intranet usage; also employ advanced tracking systems, surveys and user tests.

Answer to question on page 17

B | What gets measured gets done.

A

Communicating Change

What song lyric best describes the typical change message?

A | "Ch-ch-ch-ch-changes...Time may change me, but I can't trace time." *David Bowie*

B | "Gonna change my way of thinking, make myself a different set of rules." *Bob Dylan*

C | "Changes in latitudes, changes in attitudes, nothing remains quite the same." *Jimmy Buffet*

D | "A change would do you good. A change would do you good." *Sheryl Crow*

E | All of the above

For answer, see page 32

Avoid Too Much Information

When communicating a major change initiative, there are common best practices:

- Leverage dialogue to drive information.
- Communicate in a variety of ways.
- Involve leaders and managers.
- Don't communicate too much too soon.

Wait, what was that last one?

It may sound contrary to what you've heard, but part of the delicate art of communicating change is understanding when NOT to communicate.

Making change relevant

Whenever you communicate change, put it in context for employees:

- **Referencing previous change** and/or the past. Is this an outgrowth of something that was done before, or is it a completely new direction?
- **Linking the message** to what's important—your organization's goals, values, strategy, etc.
- Articulating **what it means for each employee** in his/her job. Here's where you'll need managers to translate change messages for their teams.

Generally, in the early phases of a change initiative, there is a lot of work going on to analyze the problem and come up with a solution. That solution then may take weeks, or even months, to implement. While the project team working on the change initiative is eager to communicate every step of the way, that might not be the best way to proceed.

Communicating too much information before any action is required on the part of the average employee can cause anxiety, be distracting and add to information clutter.

Right communication, right time

Here are some tips for communicating change at the right time:

Start with an overview. Once a plan is in place, just give employees an overview of what's going on. Tell employees what you've decided, that you now need to work out the plan and that they probably won't hear much about the project for a few months. The first thing on employees' minds will be personal impact. Be honest and outline possible scenarios and how a decision will be reached.

Make sure everything is operational before announcing. In the case of new software or technology rollouts, wait until user testing is complete to announce the launch. Otherwise, you'll face the dilemma of one company that announced new software was coming four times before the final version actually hit people's desktops. The stops and starts were confusing and stressful to employees, and by the time the new software was rolled out, no one wanted to use it for fear that it wouldn't work.

Wait until people have to take action. Most employees have a dozen or more issues that need their attention immediately. Communicating something too far in advance of when they need to act on it adds to information overload and causes them to lose focus.

Use E-mail to Communicate Major Change

For many organizations, e-mail has become the vehicle of choice when communicating big change news. And e-mail is a smart way to quickly disseminate information. But to engage employees, to help them learn about change and to build new beliefs and behaviors, communication needs to involve as well as inform.

E-mail is often the default when we have big news to communicate. There's nothing faster, and it's hard not to

How to e-mail

To use e-mail to announce major news, follow these tips:

- **Keep the message simple and brief.**
- **Set up town hall meetings** or other big gatherings to provide a forum, and/or equip managers and supervisors to meet with employees in small groups to talk more. Describe the communication process in the announcement e-mail.
- **Then focus on your real challenge:** getting leaders and managers to have face-to-face conversations with employees as soon as possible, so they can understand what the change means to them.

leverage technology when you need to reach hundreds or thousands of employees spread across the map. The problem is that these e-mails are:

- Impersonal
- Cautious and vague, to protect the company if the e-mail gets forwarded outside
- One-way

Ideally, you want to encourage face-to-face dialogue when communicating a major change. So e-mail should be the starting point to stimulate dialogue, not the first and only way change is communicated.

Make employees active participants

The more actively employees get involved in change communication, the more likely they are to become engaged in the change. Here are two suggestions for eliciting involvement:

1 | **Solicit feedback on a regular basis.** Conduct a variety of informal and formal assessments to gather employees' feedback about the change plan.

After you've gathered feedback, take visible action. This demonstrates that you value employees' input and involvement. Tell employees what you've learned and describe what is going to change as a result of their feedback.

2 | **Create ongoing participation mechanisms.** For instance, put together an informal panel of employees from different parts of the company to advise on communication-related issues.

9 Common Mistakes in Crafting Change Messages

Communicators work hard to craft employee messages about company goals, strategies, initiatives and other issues, spending countless hours to make sure messages are clear, complete and simple, but not simplistic. So it's no wonder that we're disappointed when employees don't get the message. The problem is, no matter how well we write, we keep making mistakes that undermine our efforts.

Top three mistakes and how to fix them

1. **Writing from the top down.** A brand-name company we won't mention has a monthly employee newsletter that's filled with content the CEO wants to communicate, written in language that appeals to MBAs, and framed from a 30,000-foot, corporate-headquarters perspective. There's nothing wrong with the newsletter, really, as long as it's only distributed to the 15 people in the executive suite for whom it's written. But the company prints 50,000 copies of the publication and sends it to all employees, who glance at it politely, wondering what the heck it has to do with them.

2. **Including the kitchen sink.** Where did we get the idea that we need to mention every little detail in every communication? It's just too much, especially

when "simple" e-mail announcements run to three screens, when electronic newsletters have as much content as a book, and when a print publication looks like a sea of words. The solution: Cut it down and cut (lots of stuff) out.

3. **Emphasizing the features, not the benefits.** If you've ever taken a marketing course, you may remember that one of the fundamental rules is to "sell the benefits, not the features." That means writing the ad in a way that emphasizes not what the product does, but what it will do for the target buyer.

   How does this relate to articulating employee messages? We need to stop enumerating facts and start concentrating on impact. That's what employees want to know, anyway. Why not give it to them?

Make messages meaningful

- **Get great data on your employee audience.** This starts with demographics—age groups, job categories, lengths of tenure, languages, levels of education, etc.—and includes communication preferences and needs.
- **Analyze this information to build your message strategy.** Base it on: What do employees value? What will catch their attention? How can you write so they see themselves in the story?
- **Always write with the employee in mind.** Imagine you're sending a personal message to the guy on the assembly line in your Topeka factory or to the gal processing claims in Tuscaloosa.
- **Get feedback from employees** to make sure you're on the right track, make any necessary adjustments, and measure your effectiveness (to make the case next time).

3 things to remember about communicating change:

1. **Don't communicate too much too soon**—wait to share information about change until there's something significant to talk about.

2. **Use e-mail** as one channel for sharing news about change, but not as the predominant way you communicate.

3. **Write messages about change that are geared to what employees need to hear**, not what leaders want to say.

Answer to question on page 25

D | "A change would do you good.
A change would do you good."
Sheryl Crow

A

Helping Leaders & Managers Communicate

Which of the following famous leaders in history is *not* a good role model for how leaders should communicate?

A | King Arthur

B | President Lincoln

C | Prime Minister Churchill

D | General Eisenhower

E | Colonel Sanders

For answer, see page 40

10

Help Leaders Answer Questions More Effectively

Want to create more employee participation? A key ingredient is the ability of leaders to engage employees in two-way communication. In fact, how well leaders answer questions can mean the difference between encouraging employees to speak freely and shutting people down. Here's how to coach your leaders to be more successful, whether answering questions in a large-group venue or responding to feedback in a one-on-one encounter.

1. **Clarify leaders' role as responder.** So much emphasis is placed on presentations that it's no wonder that leaders get the mistaken impression that their communication responsibility ends with the last Microsoft® Office PowerPoint® slide. But the truth is that employees feel that the presentation is just the show—it's how the leader responds to questions that really engages employees in the content.

   Leaders need to understand how important questions and answers are to the success of communication. One way to get this on a leader's radar screen is to clarify leaders' communication roles by describing expectations about how leaders should respond to questions.

Q & A

2. **Prepare leaders with answers.** The hardest questions for leaders to deal with are those they don't know how to answer. That's why a tried-and-true tool—a document with Frequently Asked Questions (and their answers)—is an effective technique for nearly every routine issue. One pitfall to avoid when creating FAQs is to omit questions that are too hard or for which the answers are not known. Leaders need a response to these types of questions (even if the response is, "We don't know.") even more than they do for questions that have factual answers.

3. **Help leaders stimulate dialogue.** It may seem counterintuitive, but the least effective way to begin a Q&A session is by saying, "Does anyone have any questions?" This question sets the expectation that only people who don't understand something that has been shared will speak up. And that puts employees in the role of students, not smart participants.

   Instead, coach leaders to try a different approach. Try, "Based on what I've just told you, what will be the hardest aspects to accomplish?" This approach creates two-way communication in a way that makes people more comfortable about participating.

Hold a rehearsal

For emotional or difficult issues, leaders may need more extensive preparation. In those cases, take a cue from politicians and executives who need to deal with the media by holding a mock Q&A session. Create the toughest questions you can think of—the real busters—and develop honest answers. Then role-play with the leader to give him or her an opportunity to rehearse.

11

Support Remote Managers in Their Role

If your workforce is spread out across the country (or countries), location managers are vital to effective communication. Whether they head a warehouse, distribution center, manufacturing facility or store, these managers are the most important source of communication and context for remote employees. Location managers set priorities, give feedback and recognize success. How can you help location managers communicate more effectively? The first step is to define their communication role.

Defining communication roles

Ideally, communicators should partner with HR to align communication roles with location managers' job description. Here are some key points to consider as you define communication roles:

What types of information should location managers communicate?

Examples:

- Translate the company's strategy for his/her location—"This is how the company's strategy relates to us."
- Articulate location's goals and strategies—"Let's talk about what we need to do to support the company's direction."
- Discuss location's performance results—"Here's how we're doing . . . keep up the great work."

What communication methods can location managers leverage?

Here are a few prescribed rules of the road/internal best practices to incorporate:

- Town hall/all hands meeting
- Team meetings
- Print vehicles, including bulletin boards
- E-mail announcements (if available)
- Conference calls (if available)

Why are communication roles so important?

Communication roles serve three key purposes:

1 | Help **communicators** establish communication standards throughout the organization and create a consistent experience for employees.

2 | Set the **expectation** that communication is an essential business process.

3 | Help **location managers** understand that communication isn't an extra task to complete, but something they already do on a regular basis. In addition, communication roles provide guidelines to help location managers do their job better.

Prevent Managers from Blocking Communication

Despite communicators' best efforts to provide managers with communication support, information often stops at the manager level—so managers are informed, while their employees are in the dark. What to do to break this logjam? Here's help.

For example, at a major global organization, managers and employees were asked to evaluate the effectiveness of the introduction of a new HR performance management system. One finding showed a wide gap between managers' and employees' comprehension of the initiative:

- Managers had a good grasp on how the process worked, its goals, what the impact would be, etc. And, of course, they gave themselves high marks for how they communicated this information to employees.
- However, information had not reached employees; most thought the program was designed for an entirely different purpose than intended. The dearth of information made them anxious and skeptical.

What can be done in the future to avoid a block?

Here are some tips:

1. **Persist when managers push back.** Managers almost universally claim they know how to communicate and don't need additional training. But the reality is most managers were promoted to their level because of their other skills—they were a great lab tech or a highly capable accountant. Communication isn't instinctive and training will almost always be beneficial.

2. **Conduct training closer to the time you need managers to communicate.** A common mistake occurs when communication training is held several months before managers have to do anything with the information. The time lag can be problematic because managers don't think about what they need to do again until they get the go-ahead to move forward. By then, they've often forgotten some of what they learned.

3. **Use the intranet to help managers build relevant skills.** Leverage the intranet to provide learning that managers can experience at their own pace. Put communication tips, case studies and other learning materials online and drive managers there during the times they need to communicate.

Why does communication frequently break down at the manager level?

- **Managers often do not recognize the value** of communication training and say they don't need it.

- **Managers believe** that if they spend five minutes with employees and pass out relevant materials, their communication role is done. In reality, more dialogue is often needed to increase employees' understanding.

3 things to remember about helping leaders and managers communicate:

1. **Coach leaders on the importance of answering questions**, and prepare them for success in making Q&A sessions engaging and meaningful.

2. **Define the communication role of remote location managers**, so they understand their importance in setting context and being the face of leadership to their employees.

3. **Use your intranet to provide learning and information for managers**, to set them up for communication success.

Answer to question on page 33

E | Colonel Sanders. But he made really good fried chicken.

A

Creating Effective Print & Electronic Communication

Which of the following is *not* true about how people use the Internet every day?

A | 58% use e-mail

B | 25% check the weather

C | 35% get news

D | 67% visit dilbert.com

E | 24% do research for their job

For answer, see page 48

Keep Pace
with Today's Trends

Do you know anyone who is trapped in the 1980s? Perhaps they still drive a Camaro Z28, wear bell bottoms and go break-dancing on Saturday nights.

Is being stuck in the past also a problem for your internal vehicles? For instance, how much has your print publication changed during the past 10 or even 20 years? Have your electronic vehicles kept pace with the rapid developments in e-communication? Because employees are avid consumers of external media, their expectations are that internal vehicles will

Sell the value of your vehicles

If employees had to pay to subscribe to one of your vehicles, what would you do differently? Assume for a moment that you have to convince employees to take out their credit cards and buy what you're selling. Also assume that employees have a limited budget, so they can't subscribe to every vehicle offered.

Your first step would be to learn everything you could about how external media companies sell their wares, and apply those same techniques to attract and retain your "subscribers."

Then, you'd develop a value statement about the channel. You'd answer these subscriber questions, "Why should I pick this up or open it? Why should I read it? What will I gain? What's in it for me?" You'd make sure this statement—this mission—is acted on and shared with employees.

also be as dynamic, fast-paced and compelling. So you need to make sure you understand what employees are looking for, and help your internal vehicles keep pace.

Best practices in external media

Now more than ever, communicators are competing with external media for employees' time and attention. One of the biggest challenges is that employees have the same expectations for internal communication as they do for external media. The good news is that it's relatively easy to borrow great ideas from effective print publications and e-vehicles.

How to keep pace

- **Make it easy to navigate information.** People are no longer a passive audience. We've grown accustomed to 'surfing' not just the web, but all media; paging through magazines and flipping television channels at a rapid pace. You need to give employees that same sense of control. Look at your print publications and e-vehicles to see if they're easy to navigate, with a clear table of contents and clearly defined sections.
- **Make internal communication interactive.** Whether instant-messaging friends, surfing the Internet or online gaming, people are controlling their media experience. Explore ways that you can make internal communication more interactive, such as blogs, online message boards, etc. In addition, provide opportunities to personalize and customize information, and solicit employees' feedback, questions and concerns.
- **Make content relevant and useful.** Employees aren't interested in reading about abstract and obscure concepts that don't directly affect them. Instead, they want information that has personal meaning. Help employees understand key issues so they can see where they fit and know how to make a contribution.

14

Leveraging the Power of Print

What's the prognosis for the role of print publications in employee communication? To borrow from Mark Twain, the reports of print's death have been greatly exaggerated. In fact, despite the proliferation of electronic vehicles, print has—and will continue to have—an important role in communicating to employees.

In the last two decades, print's star has risen and fallen—and risen again. Here's a (very) brief history of employee print publications:

- **1984 Print is king.** Newsletters rule.
- **1994 Print begins to falter.** Video ascends, and right behind it, e-mail, the Internet and all things electronic.
- **2004 Not so fast!** Print is resurrected, as its value is rediscovered.

In fact, as many communicators well know, print never died—it's just that in some organizations, it went on life support due to the mistaken belief that electronic was the one size that would fit every communication need. Meanwhile, out in the world of external media, print is very much alive: Titles and readership of magazines are increasing, direct mail continues to be an important and viable force, and even newspapers, which are struggling, are still viable. Marketers know that using a mix of media, including print, helps ensure that you reach all audience segments.

Print remains an important vehicle in organizational communication because it offers equal access (no worries about wired vs. non-wired employees), provides great at-a-glance context, is portable and user-friendly, and excels at providing details for in-depth study.

Punch up print

Despite the potential of print, many internal print publications are stuck in time; they haven't changed much in the past 10, 20, even 30 years, even while external media have become much more dynamic. Here are three tips for punching up your print publications to make them as powerful as possible:

- **Make them service-oriented.** Write not from the corporate perspective, but from the viewpoint of employees. Make it your mission to help employees understand key issues so they can see where they fit and know how to make a contribution. Think "how-to" and "news you can use."

- **Leverage visuals.** Follow best practices of external magazines to tell your stories through photographs, charts, graphs and other lively visuals. The most powerful visual of all? People's faces.

- **Give employees the choice of skimming or reading.** Depending on their interest in the topic, some of your readers will just scan—looking quickly at the headline, subheads, photo captions and sidebars—while others will devour every word. Make sure your content is chunked out to appeal to both casual skimmers and avid readers.

Find Out Why Employees Aren't Using Your Intranet

It may be hard to believe, but all it takes for site users to abandon your intranet is one solitary flaw. It's the same principle as finding a fly in your soup: It can spoil the whole bowl. Through the years, we've seen a number of "flies in the soup" that keep employees from using their company's intranet. Here are five:

1. **Inconsistent design.** A uniform look and feel is the most fundamental principle of intranet design. You want site visitors to experience similar structure, as well as consistent and intuitive navigation, as they browse from page to page. Without consistent design, you're also missing out on a valuable opportunity to develop a strong brand.

2. **Outdated content.** Stale content is STILL the number one reason employees don't visit their organization's intranet. (Will we ever learn?) It really makes perfect sense. Imagine visiting CNN.com today and reading the headline: "Saddam Hussein Captured." Chances are, you would find an alternate source for up-to-date news.

3. **Badly organized information.** Physical organization is a problem plaguing many corporate intranets. Quite often, a file and folder structure is used (think "corporate silos") instead of logical organization: structuring the site in such a way that promotes logical workflow. The key is to figure out what employees need and build information to suit their needs.

Good example:

http://www.apple.com clearly makes it a priority to maintain a consistent look and feel throughout its site, and definitely achieves strong brand recognition.

Good example:

http://howstuffworks.com, a site that explains how everything around us works, from technology to nature, does a good job at writing in layman's terms, making it relevant for all audiences.

4. **Content that's not audience focused.** It's easy to post press releases, shareholder updates and product information on your homepage as a way to make content seem "fresh." While your intentions may be good, you're not fooling anyone. Employees want information that's relevant to them, not company executives, shareholders, consumers or the competition. This isn't to say that you can't adapt existing content for your intranet. Just make sure you answer employees' big question, "What does this mean to me?"

5. **Poor search engine.** Finding information on your intranet shouldn't be a game of hide and seek. An intranet needs to have a search function that allows employees to find the information they're looking for. This is especially important for large intranet sites so packed with information that it's hard to decide where to start a search.

Good example:

http://careerbuilder.com allows you to perform a job search based on a variety of search criteria including company name, keywords, job category, title and location. You can narrow down your results by selecting additional search criteria.

Intranet fundamentals

1 | Use intuitive/logical navigation and structure.

2 | Keep the copy short (and update it often).

3 | Make graphic design work for you.

4 | Make your intranet interactive.

3 things to remember about print and electronic communication:

1. **Make your communication vehicles easy to navigate**, so that employees can skim and scan, and quickly find the information they need.

2. **Use print for what it (still) does best:** at-a-glance information, portable, user-friendly and available to all employees equally (whether or not they have electronic access).

3. **Analyze your intranet** to make sure it doesn't contain these fatal flaws: inconsistent design, outdated content, badly organized information, irrelevant information, or a poor search engine.

Answer to question on page 41

D | We made this fact up: There is no data on Dilbert.

A

Communicating Visually

Of all the senses, vision is the most critical. Which of the following is *not* true?

A | 8% of adult males are color-blind

B | 70% of people who use computers have vision problems

C | 25% of Americans are nearsighted

D | 65% of adult males can't tell the difference between sand, taupe and beige

E | 10% of Americans are farsighted

For answer, see page 56

Leverage Visuals to Communicate Complex Ideas

Got a complex message you need to communicate? The more technical and multi-layered the concept is, the more you need visuals to create interest and understanding. Whether you're communicating about an intricate process change, or presenting complicated data, visuals can simplify your ideas and make it quick and easy for employees to grasp key information.

Most adults are visual learners by nature. If you want information to be more than just data, then you need to create learning; visuals will stimulate learning.

What is a visual?

Quite simply, a visual is anything that is seen by the eyes, as opposed to being heard. Flipcharts, handouts, posters, projections and Microsoft® Office PowerPoint® slides, if used correctly, are all considered visuals.

Visuals are especially valuable when communicating to non-wired employees in the retail, manufacturing and transportation industries. Without electronic media such as e-mail or the intranet, reaching these employees can be a real challenge. Visuals ensure that your messages are getting through to everyone.

How do I leverage visuals to enhance my communication?

When deciding how to use visuals, try to pinpoint situations when a visual could enhance (not simply outline or summarize) your message and provide further context for employees.

Some situations when visuals are especially beneficial include:

- **Communicating technological system or process changes.** The "domino effect" created by these changes touches employees in various departments and divisions and often changes the way they've done their work for years. Visuals can communicate what will be different, why the change is occurring and what new behaviors are expected.
- **Presenting complex data.** Numbers on paper are never as effective as graphs, tables and charts. Use visuals to tell a story and allow employees to draw obvious conclusions. For example, if a line graph shows that employee morale is low when company productivity is low, the obvious conclusion, that low productivity = low morale, can be reached with a minimal number of words.

- **Reinforcing ideas and beliefs.** Corporate missions, visions and values are commonly nothing more than words on paper to employees. But creating a visual that provides insight can create additional meaning.

Why use visuals?

- **Visuals can tell a whole story, faster** and with greater nuance than words. We are all busy—now more than ever. Employees want access to information that is fast and easy to digest and understand. Visuals support the need to "get it" fast.
- **Visuals are memorable.** When we attach a visual to an important message, it creates recall. We can help employees remember messages by giving them visual "handles" to grasp when trying to recall content.
- **A visual can explain the context** that makes a message more than just words. They help to make complex ideas quickly and easily understood.

17

Typeface

Put Stylized Type to Work

A number of roadblocks prevent us from making communication more visual: lack of time, a strained budget, limited access to professional designers, etc. We're often left with a sea of text that employees, with their short attention spans, are likely to ignore. But you have more control than you realize to get employees' attention. Using only your text, you can create visual interest. Here's how:

Why type matters

"Typography" is the balance and interplay of text that helps readers understand, absorb and navigate content. Page after page of dense text makes it hard for readers to cut through the thicket. But when type is used well, there is a balance—among blocks of text, headlines or subheads and the surrounding white space—that draws readers in.

Five tips for making type more visual

It's time to make friends with your formatting palette; apply these methods to Word documents, PowerPoint presentations, and e-mail to get your messages noticed.

1. **Use more than one typeface.** Varying your font is a good way to create visual contrast. Perhaps the most important rule of good typography is don't overdo it. The standard is no more than two fonts per article, but be sure to check your corporate guidelines to see if your company has a standard typeface and specific rules on usage.

2. **Make headlines and subheads bold.** Headlines and subheads indicate the hierarchy of your content. They act as starting cues indicating where sections begin and what the sections are about. Therefore, headlines and subheads should always be clearly visible. Try bold, two or more point sizes bigger than your text. If your body text is a serif, we suggest using a sans-serif font for the headline or vice-versa. If you're using all the same font style, make headlines and subheads a different color.
3. **Vary your type styles.** Use your formatting palette to emphasize words or an important sentence. **Bold** and *italic*, used together or separately, attract the eye. In a block of text, they help employees navigate the content, acting as road signs and suggesting importance. Making key words and phrases bold is an effective way to break up the monotony of straight text.
4. **Paint your article with a little bit of color.** Color isn't just for headlines. If there is a paragraph or two that you want to call attention to, apply a legible color that offers enough contrast from the rest of the text but can still be read against the background (e.g., blue, red or burgundy against a white background). Test legibility by making a photocopy of your page. If your colored text is too light, go for a darker color.
5. **Use callouts.** A callout is an easy editorial design method, used often in magazines, and a real effective way to break up copy.

Find a sentence that sums up your objective and make it four to six points bigger than the body font size. Make sure to leave adequate white space around the sentence and voila! You've got yourself a callout.

18

Use Icons
to Cut Through the Clutter

Icons are so prevalent in our day-to-day lives that we often don't even notice them as communication. For example, we intrinsically recognize that when a door has an image of a figure wearing a dress, it communicates that the room is for women. Since one simple graphic demonstrates a concept that would take many words to explain, icons can be particularly powerful in employee communication.

Using icons in employee communication

Since most of us struggle to make communication more visual, we should consider using icons as visual tools to convey key information. Here's what makes icons so powerful:

When creating your own icons—follow these guidelines:

- **Make sure they're clear.** Only very simple images make good icons. If your icon is too busy, you risk that employees won't be able to make out the image or understand it.
- **Ensure that they're without cultural bias.** Colors and images vary from culture to culture. For example, in France, an icon of a house would not represent "homepage" because the French call it a "welcome page." Before introducing icons to your organization, test them on a diverse group of employees.
- **Keep it simple.** Too many icons can add to employees' confusion. Don't overdo it.

- **Hire a designer.** Think about when and where you could leverage icons: operating principles, values, business strategies, etc. Then, enlist a designer to help you create an icon.
- **Make it easy for new employees to learn what they mean.** Don't ever take it for granted that employees know what different icons represent. Whether in print or online, include a key that offers an explanation of each icon.

What are icons?

An icon is a small, easy-to-recognize image that (if well designed and thought out) is universally understood. Most icons are one-dimensional and one color, and their style can vary from realistic to abstract.

- **They're widely applicable.** A well-designed icon has the same meaning globally, offering a rich potential for communicating across language barriers. For example, let's say that safety is a corporate priority for your organization; an icon of a hardhat would be universally understood.
- **They cut through the clutter.** Between all the words in print and online, an icon stands out like a beacon in the night to help readers navigate, guiding them to various kinds of content. On a subscription website, a "key" icon represents premium content, so if you're a member, you'll be able to access in-depth content.
- **They create recall.** Some organizations use icons to represent key information, like company values. By nature, adults are visual learners. Icons serve as "handles" that employees can grasp when trying to recall information.

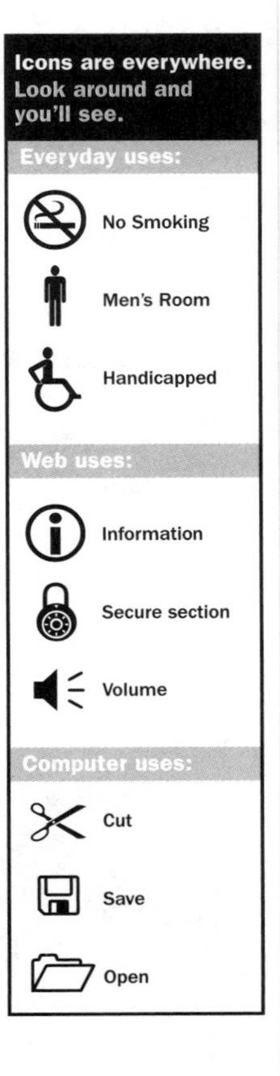

3 things to remember about communicating visually:

1. **Use visuals to tell an entire story at a glance**, especially when you have a diverse workforce.
2. **Employ typography techniques** as the cheapest and easiest way to make your communication more visual.
3. **Create clear, simple icons** to cut through communication clutter.

Answer to question on page 49

D | While it may actually be true, no studies have verified this observation.

A

Strengthening the Communication Function

In terms of communicators' professional development, what is the most effective way to learn new skills?

A | Read a book

B | Take an online course

C | Go to a workshop or seminar

D | Take one long nap a day

E | Learn by doing

For answer, see page 64

19

Create an Organizational Structure that Supports Your Objectives

If you've ever wondered whether or not your function is staffed and structured in the most logical and effective way, you're not alone. The truth is, the "right" structure is a moving target that depends on the current needs and priorities of your organization. Different approaches work at different companies. Further, different structures may work at different points in time.

To determine if you have the right structure in place, think about how your business is changing and what your goals are. Periodically ask the following questions to see how your function stacks up:

- **Does the most senior person in your function serve as your advocate?** It doesn't really matter if you report into Corporate Communication, Public Affairs, Human Resources or Marketing as long as the senior person you're reporting to values employee communication and acts as an advocate of it to senior management.
- **Are you able to support the needs of your internal clients and stakeholders?** Do you have enough resources in place to meet your organization's internal communication needs? There's no magic number, but if your dispersed organization is going through a major change initiative that requires extensive resources and you have a team of five people in one location, you probably need to make a change.

- **Are you close enough to your customers to know what their needs are?** Your customers are employees. Do you have people "on the ground" in key locations (plants, regional offices, etc.) to understand the mindset of employees and address their needs?
- **Do you have problems creating alignment throughout your organization?** Your reporting structure—whether centralized, decentralized, a matrix, or some combination of the three—is irrelevant so long as that structure fosters the collaboration, networking and alignment you need to meet your goals. You should also think about linkages between your team and other key groups, such as HR, OD, etc.

Once you've considered how your organization's needs stack up against your function's structure and staffing, you'll need ammunition to take to senior management if you want to get anything changed.

Benchmark the best

Consider doing a benchmarking study of other companies to see how you stack up against them. Some things to consider when benchmarking:

- **Industry isn't the most important criteria.** Instead, choose organizations that are similar to yours in terms of size, scope and geographical set up. However, if you're a manufacturing company, try to include at least a couple other manufacturers in your study.
- **Be considerate of people's time.** Keep your questionnaire short and focused on what you need to learn and do any background research (such as number of employees, locations, etc.) ahead of time.
- **In exchange for their time,** send participants a copy of your findings and be willing to share information about your organization with them.

Restore Order with Communication Standards

Does your company's communication culture resemble the Wild West? Do outlaw communicators make up their own rules about what to say and who to say it to? Are employees feeling conflicted and uncertain about who or what to believe? If so, it's time to restore order. The first step is establishing communication standards.

Why are communication standards important?

Three outcomes of implementing communication standards are:

1 | **Consistency**. All employees, regardless of job function or location, have a shared communication experience.

2 | **Accountability.** Communication becomes a "need to do" instead of "nice to do."

3 | **Community.** Individuals support each other to enhance communication throughout their local business unit and the company as a whole.

Examples

Sample communication standards:

- **Local communicators** provide facility managers with resources needed (e.g., PowerPoint presentations, talking points) to conduct quarterly town hall meetings.
- **All intranet pages** have a standard design template and navigation structure.
- **Each business unit** conducts an annual communication assessment using a standard measurement tool.

How can communicators establish standards?

The process of establishing communication standards requires collaboration with key individuals responsible for communication throughout the company. Here are some key discussion questions:

- How do we define employee communication at our company? What purpose does it serve?
- Who are the key individuals in charge of employee communication and what role do they play?
- What are some recent employee communication success stories? What made them successful?
- What challenges are we facing? What can we do to overcome these challenges?
- What are two or three expectations we need to set for how communication occurs in our company? How will we communicate these expectations?

What are communication standards?

The purpose of communication standards isn't to impose rigid guidelines, but to set expectations for how communication should occur across your company. Just as the Wild West wasn't tamed in a day, the process of setting communication standards takes time and effort, but the end result is well worth it.

Establish a Communicators Network

A significant challenge for communicators is ensuring that employees everywhere receive and have equal access to essential information. One of the most efficient, cost-effective solutions is to develop a communicators network.

Networks help address the challenges of making communication consistent across different work sites, including:

- **Employees** are in a wide variety of positions and levels, with different access methods available to them.
- **Locations** are geographically diverse—keeping track of how sites operate on opposite sides of the world is virtually impossible.
- **Sites** frequently have their own internal organizational structures.

One example of a network's value

One possible purpose for a communicators network can be to enhance distribution of print and other communication vehicles by:

- **Having someone who is accountable** for distribution
- **Allowing for individual sites** to customize distribution processes to meet unique needs
- **Giving employees a local contact person** for questions about a communication vehicle, such as how they can submit ideas for a newsletter

Defining distribution roles

To effectively fulfill their role in helping you reach employees, network members should know:

The best method for distributing print publications for their sites, whether that be inter-office mail, desk drops, literature racks or a combination of the three

How to design an effective bulletin board—creating a clear, consistent layout so messages are easily understood by employees

When newsletters will be shipped

How quickly bulletin board updates need to be posted

Basic answers to employee questions about publications and newsletters

Where they can go to get questions answered

What is a communicators network?

A communicators network is made up of employees at sites across an organization who are responsible for facilitating communication at their locations. Network members don't need to be experienced communicators; instead, they can be employees who are interested in expanding their skills and have a desire to support improvements throughout the organization.

A network can have a variety of objectives and areas of focus. For example, it can exist to share internal best practices, to leverage learning opportunities or to create efficiencies such as negotiating a contract with a single graphic design firm instead of multiple arrangements with many firms.

3 things to remember about strengthening the communication function:

1. **Structure your department** to get close to your internal clients, and meet the needs of your "customers"—employees.

2. **Set standards** to create a consistent approach to communication throughout your organization.

3. **Establish a communicators network** to address distribution challenges.

Answer to question on page 57

E | Although all are helpful (even the nap), the best way to learn is by doing.

Index